D0624221

Meet
Nelson Mandela

by Bobbi Katz

A Bullseye Biography

Random House New York

*With special thanks to the African-American
Institute and the librarians and South Africans
who helped me gather information.*

Photo credits: AP/Wide World Photos, p. 1, 4, 19, 24, 25, 38, 41, 46, 51, 64, 67, 80, 95, 96, 97, 98, 99, 100, 101, 103, 106; Reuters/Bettmann, 48, 108; United Nations/Contact, 33.

A BULLSEYE BOOK PUBLISHED BY RANDOM HOUSE, INC.

Cover design by Fabia Wargin Design and Creative Media Applications, Inc.
Copyright © 1995 by Bobbi Katz
Map copyright © 1995 by Random House, Inc.
All rights reserved under International and Pan-American Copyright Conventions.
Published in the United States by Random House, Inc., New York, and simultaneously
in Canada by Random House of Canada Limited, Toronto.

Library of Congress Cataloging-in-Publication Data
Katz, Bobbi.
Meet Nelson Mandela / by Bobbi Katz.
p. cm. — (Bullseye biography.)
ISBN 0-679-87166-7 (pbk.)
1. Mandela, Nelson, 1918– —Juvenile literature. 2. Presidents—South Africa—
Biography—Juvenile literature. [1. Mandela, Nelson, 1918– . 2. Blacks—
South Africa—Biography. 3. Civil rights workers. 4. Presidents—South Africa.
5. South Africa—Race relations.] I. Title. II. Series.
DT1949.M35K38 1995
968.06′4′092—dc20
[B] 94-34178

Manufactured in the United States of America 10 9 8 7 6 5 4 3 2 1

Contents

*Nelson Mandela shows his warm smile
outside a courthouse in 1958.*

I

Elections! Elections!

During the last days of April 1994, the world held its breath. A miracle was taking place in South Africa.

For the first time in the nation's history, a democratic election was being held.

For years, only the few million white South Africans had been allowed to vote. But most South Africans are nonwhite. Millions of black people had no voice in the government of their own country.

The people began to arrive at the polling places before sunrise on the first day of the elections. There were people of all races, but most of them were black. Some of them were young, some were old. Some were sick and had to be carried to the polls on stretchers. But no one wanted to miss the chance to vote.

People waited and waited in the long lines. Some of them waited for more than ten hours in the hot sun. Children of all races played together while their parents stood in line to vote. Observers from many nations kept watch to make sure that the voting was fair.

As they waited, the new voters felt joyful and proud. But many of them were nervous, too. Some white South Africans did not want their black countrymen to vote. There was a chance that violence would break out at the polls. In the days before the elections, there had been bombings and bloodshed.

But the people were willing to risk their lives. Most of them were waiting to cast their votes for one special man—a black man—to be president of the new South Africa: Nelson Mandela.

2

A Little Boy
with a Big Name

July 18, 1918, was a happy day for Nosekeni Fanny, one of the wives of Henry Gadla Mandela. She had just given birth to her first child, a healthy boy.

The baby's great-great-grandfather was Ngubencuka, a king of the Thembu tribe. But because Nosekeni Fanny was a Christian, her baby was given both a Thembu name and a Christian name, which was the custom.

Henry and Nosekeni Fanny named their son Nelson Rolihlahla. "Rolihlahla" means "stirring up trouble" in Xhosa, the language of the Thembu. Admiral Horatio Nelson (1758–1805) was a British war hero who served his country and its people with all his heart and soul. Nelson Rolihlahla Mandela—his parents had chosen a perfect name for their son!

But when Nelson Rolihlahla grew older, his little sisters invented their own nickname for him—Buti.

Buti's family lived in the Transkei, which is a dry, hilly region of southeastern South Africa. The Transkei is a place where the sky seems endless. A special smoky smell from cooking fires hangs in the air. The Thembu people had lived in the Transkei for many years before any Europeans set foot in Africa.

Each of Henry Mandela's three wives had her own home. And each one had three *rondavel*s and a *kraal*, or shed, for goats and cattle. Rondavels are round huts with dirt floors, walls of mud brick, and roofs of woven grasses and leaves. One rondavel was used for storing clay pots and baskets of cornmeal and other supplies. Another was used for cooking. The family lived in the third rondavel, which contained simple chairs and sleeping mats.

Buti and his sisters were never lonely. They were always welcome in the rondavels of their father's other wives. And they always had half brothers and half sisters to play with or to turn to for help.

When Buti was still very young, he had the job of caring for his family's goats and cattle. He let the goats and cattle out of the kraal in the morning. He watched to make sure none of them wandered off as they grazed on the hillsides. Then he closed the animals in the kraal at the end of the day.

Buti's sisters did girls' chores. They helped their mother plant and harvest her cornfield. They learned to grind the kernels into meal between two smooth rocks.

Henry Mandela was quite well off compared to most of the people of the Transkei. But one day he became very ill. And he knew that he would not get better. How could he prepare for the future of his bright young son?

Buti was doing very well in the local school run by missionaries. His parents wanted him to have a good education. So Henry asked his nephew, who was the chief of all the Thembus, to take care of young Buti. Chief Jongintaba promised that the boy would have the best education he could provide.

When Henry died, Chief Jongintaba sent for Buti. The chief lived in Mqekezweni, which had been the home of Thembu kings for generations.

Buti packed his little metal trunk and said good-bye to his mother and his sisters. He knew that Mqekezweni was too far away for him to visit them often. How lonely he must have felt!

But one of Chief Jongintaba's wives liked

Buti right away. She treated him as if he were her own child. And her son, Justice, became a big brother to Buti.

Justice and the rest of the chief's family called Buti by his Thembu name, Rolihlahla. But he used his English name, Nelson, at school.

Nelson and Justice hunted for birds with their slingshots and roasted them on sticks. They shared the boys' chores—letting the cattle out of the kraal at daybreak and herding them back before nightfall. Like the other boys in the tribe, they attended the small school that still stands in Mqekezweni, and they went to church on Sundays.

But the boys received special treats as members of the chief's family. Sometimes they were allowed to ride the chief's horses. And, most important of all, the chief's sons served at his banquets.

When the tribe's elders came to take part in tribal councils, three rondavels were built and joined together to make a royal banquet hall. The tribal elders dined with the chief.

While he served the food and drink, Nelson listened to every word that was said. In school he was learning geography, English, and history. But the history he learned in Chief Jongintaba's dining hall was very different from the history he learned in school.

The missionaries who ran the school spoke only of the brave white pioneers who brought Christianity to Africa. They did not teach the children about the rich history of the African people or about the old system of government and trade. They did not speak of the African poems and folktales that were passed from one generation to another.

But Nelson heard the elders talk about the many different tribes and clans that had once lived happily in southern Africa. They talked about a time, before the coming of the white men, when Africans ruled themselves and were free. As he listened, Nelson learned of the brave chiefs and heroic deeds that were part of his peoples' history.

When Thembu boys were about sixteen, they became men. The elders taught them the unwritten laws they would need to know in order to take part in tribal courts.

The British did not interfere with local justice. Whenever there was a problem in the tribe, the elders asked many questions and acted as judges. They made decisions with the help of the tribal council. Violence and serious crimes were very rare.

Young Nelson was fascinated by the tribal courts. And he was fascinated by the elders' stories. But he couldn't help wondering: Why had everything changed so much? What had happened to the old Africa, the old way of life?

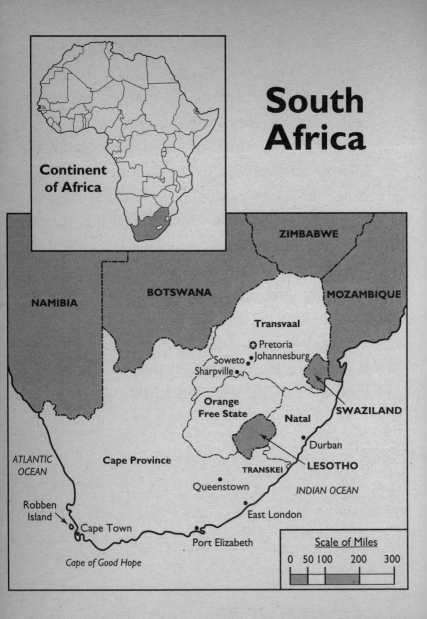

South Africa

Continent of Africa

ZIMBABWE

NAMIBIA

BOTSWANA

MOZAMBIQUE

Transvaal

⊛ Pretoria
Soweto • • Johannesburg
Sharpville •

Orange
Free State

Natal

SWAZILAND

ATLANTIC
OCEAN

Cape Province

Durban

TRANSKEI

LESOTHO

Queenstown •

INDIAN OCEAN

Robben
Island

East London •

Cape Town •

Port Elizabeth

Cape of Good Hope

Scale of Miles

0 50 100   200   300

3

A Strange Post Office

Hundreds of years ago, ships sailing from Europe passed around the tip of Africa on their way to India and the Far East. Sailors set up a post office there, leaving letters under marked stones. Returning ships would pick them up and deliver them to Europe.

In 1652 the Dutch established a trading post at the tip of Africa. They called it the Cape Colony. The post provided fresh meat and produce to the Dutch ships.

The native people living there were dark-skinned hunters and shepherds. The Dutch called them Hottentots. These people refused to work for the Dutch, who treated them badly. The trading company decided to bring in slaves and convict labor from Asia.

Soon more settlers arrived. Many of them wanted to become farmers, or *Boers,* as they are called in Dutch. At first the Africans were willing to share their land with the new settlers. But the native Africans did not have the same ideas about owning land as the Europeans. They did not build fences and say, "This land belongs to me." They farmed their land and grazed their flocks as a group.

The Boers did not try to understand the Africans' culture. They took their land and even tried to make the Africans their slaves.

The Africans fought back. Sometimes they were successful. But in the end, the tribesmen's spears and bravery were no match for the Boers' guns.

The British began to settle on the Cape in 1820. Soon many more British settlers, drawn by the good climate, started arriving.

The Boers didn't like anything about the British. The newcomers spoke another language, English, and seemed to be taking over everything with their unfamiliar ways.

To the horror of the Dutch settlers, the British gave equal rights to nonwhites. They even outlawed slavery.

Between 1835 and 1843, thousands of Boers began to move inland. This was called the Great Trek. They had many battles with native tribes along the way. The Xhosa, the Nguni, the Sotho, and the Zulu all tried to stop them. In one battle 3,000 Zulus were cut down by Boer bullets. The river ran red with Zulu blood. To this day it is called the Blood River.

The trekkers moved on. They crossed the Vaal River and established the South African Republic, which is now the Transvaal. They called themselves Afrikaners, and said they were "the white tribe of Africa."

At first the British had little interest in the new Afrikaner states. But when diamonds and gold were discovered, the British took over all of South Africa. And in 1902, the country was made part of the British Empire. It was called the Union of South Africa.

There were still problems within the country's borders. The Boers and the British remained bitter enemies. Asians and people of mixed race had few rights. And within the new government, the black Africans now had next to no rights.

The British had promised black Africans voting rights. After all, black Africans had served as loyal soldiers during the British wars with the Afrikaners. But the new constitution gave voting rights only to those blacks living in the Cape. And they could vote only for white people.

In 1912 a group of Africans joined together to work for black rights. Their organization later became the African National Congress. The ANC's first president was John Dube, a Zulu of noble birth. The treasurer, Pixley Ka I. Seme, was a lawyer. Both

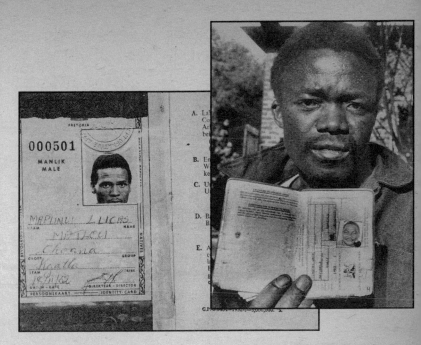

A South African passbook (left). The government forced nonwhites to carry one at all times. A Johannesburg resident showing his passbook (right).

men had gone to college in the United States. The ANC offered to help the government work out black grievances.

The very next year the government adopted the Natives' Land Act. This law kept blacks from buying land outside small areas set aside for blacks.

But this created a problem. Who would mine the gold and build the railroads? The government decided to start a pass system. With passes, the blacks could go only where their services were needed. They could no longer move freely through the land of their ancestors.

This was the world in which Nelson Mandela grew up.

4

The Road to the Golden City

Chief Jongintaba kept his promise to Nelson's father. He provided his bright young cousin with the best possible education. Luckily, the chief had a car—a prized possession in those days. So when Nelson finished the local elementary school, the chief drove him to an advanced school in the town of Qokolweni.

A few years later, Nelson entered Clarkebury, a Methodist high school in Engcobo. He graduated from high school with high marks. The proud chief gave a great feast to celebrate his graduation. And there was more than one reason to celebrate. Nelson was going to college! The whole village was very proud of him.

The chief gave Nelson a brand-new three-piece suit and a pair of shiny new shoes. Nelson Mandela was on his way to a brand-new life.

It was at Fort Hare College that Nelson discovered his lifelong passion—politics. He also made friends with whom he could discuss the many ideas that were on his mind.

But Nelson's new life did not last long. A small disagreement had developed between the students and the people in charge of the college.

Nelson saw his first opportunity for political action. He and some of his friends started to organize student groups which would fight for students' rights. The people who ran Fort Hare did not like this. They didn't want troublemakers around. They asked Nelson and his friends to leave the school.

Chief Jongintaba was very angry. Nelson had disgraced his clan by returning without a college degree. The chief urged him to apologize to the college officials. But Nelson said no. He felt he had done nothing wrong.

The chief believed he knew what was best for Nelson. He decided it was time for Nelson to marry. He had already chosen a wife for him and had paid the traditional price of cattle and money to the bride's father. And, as was the custom, he had *not* consulted Nelson. Everyone in Mqekezweni was getting ready for a wedding—except the groom!

Unlike his father and the chief, Nelson was a Christian. He wanted only one wife. And he wanted a woman with whom he could share ideas and dreams. He loved the chief. He respected the traditions of the Thembu. But college had opened his mind to new ways. He could not agree to this marriage.

Nelson talked to Justice. They decided to flee together to the city of Johannesburg. Jo'burg, as the South Africans call it, was in

*Downtown Johannesburg, where Nelson
first worked and attended college.*

the center of the gold-mining region. It was
the biggest and busiest city in the country.

Nelson and Justice knew that a Thembu
worked at the Crown mines. They were sure
they could count on his help. But soon after
Justice and Nelson reached the "Golden
City," a furious Chief Jongintaba tracked
them down. He ordered the young men to
come home.

Justice obeyed, but Nelson asked the chief
to let him stay in Jo'burg to work and study.
He wanted to become a lawyer. That way he
could carry on in the spirit of the tribal coun-

cils. Chief Jongintaba finally agreed. But he told Nelson he would have to earn his own living.

Nelson knew that life in the city would not be easy. While blacks could work in Jo'burg, they could not live there. Black townships had sprung up around the city. They were crowded, ugly places with rows of tiny houses. Most houses did not have running water or toilets.

Nelson found a job with a small business that tried to find homes for blacks. The pay was barely enough to live on. But Nelson was lucky. He found a room outside the

Soweto, a part of Johannesburg most white people never see—except from a tour bus such as this one.

city in the township of Alexandra.

Nelson made new friends. One person he met through work was Walter Sisulu, a law student. Sisulu had a black mother and a white father.

Walter and Nelson were both interested in politics, and Walter was a member of the ANC. The two young men became such good friends that Nelson soon moved into the house Walter shared with his mother.

To Nelson's delight, he discovered that his college friends Oliver Tambo and Congress Mbata were also working in Jo'burg. They urged Nelson to become part of a group of young black people with new ideas for their country.

In 1942, Nelson completed college. Now he was ready to start law school at the University of the Witwatersrand. This time it was Walter who bought Nelson a new suit. He also introduced him to a white lawyer, Lazer Sidelsky, who hired Nelson as a law clerk.

Mr. Sidelsky treated Nelson as an equal.

But one day when Nelson was dictating a letter to a white secretary, an important white client arrived. Embarrassed, the secretary pretended that Nelson was a messenger. She even tried to give him a tip! Nelson was very angry. But at the time he was too busy with law school to worry much about what had happened.

At the university, Nelson joined the International Club. It was there that students from India introduced him to the teachings of Mahatma Gandhi. Gandhi was a leader who believed that nonviolent protest was the best way to change unjust laws. The more Nelson learned about Gandhi, the more he liked his ideas.

Nelson's circle of friends grew even larger. And he began to see the possibilities of people of all races working together for a better South Africa.

Little did Nelson Mandela and his friends realize that life in South Africa would soon grow much worse.

5

A Time to Build

Nelson continued to work and study law. He kept fit by jogging each morning and boxing when he found time. The Sisulu's home buzzed with visitors, laughter, and interesting talk. There was always room for a few extra people who needed a place to stay.

One of those people was Walter's cousin Evelyn. Evelyn was a nurse. When she met Nelson, she felt there was something very special about him. Nelson felt the same way about her. Soon he and Evelyn decided to marry.

While the young couple waited for a house of their own, they lived with Evelyn's sister and brother-in-law. The Mandelas' first son, Thembi, was born in 1945. The happy father visited the hospital with new nightgowns for his wife and an armload of baby clothes.

The family was assigned a two-room house by the government. At last they had a place of their own!

Nelson was a modern father. He helped Evelyn by bathing the baby and doing the shopping. He also made sure that his sister Leabie received a good education. She came to live with the couple to attend high school.

Then Nosekeni Fanny fell ill. Nelson brought his mother to his township for medical care. She gradually got better and continued to stay on with Evelyn and Nelson. Nosekeni Fanny was a big help with their growing family.

A second son, Makgatho, was born in 1950. Four years later, a daughter, Makaziwe, arrived. Everyone called her Maki.

Evelyn continued to work as a nurse. Nelson was still working part-time and attending law school. Yet both of them found time for politics.

Evelyn was active in the nursing union. The union was trying to get equal pay for black nurses. As in every other kind of job in South Africa, nonwhite nurses earned much less than white nurses for the same work.

Nelson had joined the ANC in 1944. When World War II was over, he marched with other ANC members in the victory parade. Among the ANC flags was a banner that read, LET'S FINISH THE JOB! People of color in South Africa wanted the freedom and liberty for which World War II had been fought.

During and after World War II, most white South Africans were horrified by Germany's racial policies. The Nazis killed millions of Jews and Gypsies and other groups of people they considered inferior to their own "pure" race. South Africans rallied to defeat the Germans. But many South African whites seemed blind to the racism they lived with right at home.

Many of the younger ANC members felt their organization wasn't responding to the times. A group of them, including Nelson Mandela, Walter Sisulu, and Oliver Tambo, started the ANC Youth League in 1944. The Youth League argued that blacks outnumbered all other racial groups. The country had been their land for centuries. They wanted black culture to be recognized.

While Nelson treasured many tribal values, he questioned some of these ideas. He was against making any one racial group more important than any other. Nevertheless, he was elected secretary of the Youth League.

Meanwhile, many white South Africans were growing uneasy. In 1947 the United Nations had spoken out against the country's racial policies. Some whites wanted a more democratic government. But others feared that their way of life would be in danger if they gave the nonwhite majority a say.

In 1948, the conservative National Party won a surprise victory in the South African elections. The party was helped to power by a group called the *Broederbond,* or Brotherhood. Its members took an oath to preserve the Afrikaner way of life. Their goals were the same as those of their Boer ancestors, who had made the Great Trek. By the 1940s, the Broederbond was rich and powerful.

There was little freedom for nonwhites before the National Party took over. Now a new and even more frightening era began: the era of apartheid. *Apartheid* means "separateness" in the Afrikaners' language, Afrikaans.

The basis of apartheid was fear. Its purpose was to keep all the races separate and the whites in power in South Africa. Over the years, 3,000 pages of apartheid laws were written. And in the name of apartheid, terrible cruelties were inflicted on the people of South Africa. While the blacks suffered the most, white South Africans also suffered in less obvious ways.

In the South African city of Durban, a sign restricted use of a beach to whites.

Apartheid defined people as White, Asian, Colored (mixed-race), and Bantu (black). It divided the country into areas reserved for each group. Passbook laws became stricter and more complicated. Strikes by black workers were banned. Under the Bantu Education Bill, elementary school was declared unnecessary for black children. The missionary schools were closed.

Apartheid was building a wall between the different peoples of South Africa. The National Party kept adding new bricks to that wall to make it higher and stronger. Mandela and the ANC vowed to do their best to create doors and windows in it.

6

Cells with Invisible Bars

The National Party victory convinced Nelson, the ANC, and other groups working for civil liberties that they needed to act fast. The government was continuing to pass new laws and restrictions. The ANC quickly elected Oliver Tambo and Walter Sisulu to high positions. Then they brought in Nelson Mandela.

The ANC was ready to use every peaceful method to gain basic human rights for all peoples in South Africa. But what would work best?

The new ANC leaders realized that the

country depended on black workers to mine its diamonds and gold. It also needed them to raise its sugar and wheat. The ANC began to plan a strike for black workers. Refusing to work would show the government they meant business.

But before the ANC announced its plan, the Communist Party and the South African Indian Congress, another political group in South Africa, called for a day of protest against the new laws. The date was set for May 1, 1950, in Johannesburg.

Mandela later called that day a turning point in his life. Black workers gave enormous support to the peaceful protest. But police fired on the demonstrators. They killed eighteen people and wounded many others. Nelson saw that there were whites and Asians as well as blacks among the victims. Once again, he was convinced that anti-apartheid groups of all races should work together.

ANC officials wrote to South Africa's

prime minister, Daniel Malan, in 1951. They stated their belief in equal rights for all South Africans. The situation, they said, had become one of life and death. The ANC officials warned that they would start a nonviolent campaign on April 6, 1952, unless the government took steps toward democracy.

The prime minister's secretary wrote back to the ANC. The letter said that the differences between the races were not manmade and could never be changed. The letter also told the ANC to send its messages to the minister of native affairs in the future. The door to understanding had been slammed shut.

The ANC and its allies decided to mark April 6, 1952, the three-hundred-year anniversary of the founding of the Cape Colony, in their own way. They began a Defiance of Unjust Laws Campaign. They also continued with their plans for a national strike. It was set for June 26, 1952.

The Defiance Campaign was targeted at two apartheid rules, the pass laws and the curfew. Blacks and Asians could not move freely within the country without passes. And they could be arrested if they were on the street after 11:00 P.M.

Nelson was in charge of the campaign. He traveled all over the country to drum up support for it. He was a tall, handsome man with a ready smile. People recognized him as a leader, and many agreed to help his cause.

On June 26, the strike and the campaign began. Participants started going into townships without passes. That evening Nelson Mandela himself led a peaceful group onto the street—and into waiting police vans!

Nelson and his supporters spent the night in jail. But now more and more people were breaking the pass laws and the curfew. And more and more people were joining the ANC. Soon the group swelled to over 100,000 members. Nelson hoped that the

Nelson and other ANC youth leaders in court in 1952.

government might begin to listen to them at last.

But one night about a month later, as Nelson and his family were sleeping, police surrounded their house. They burst in and arrested Nelson. This happened at the homes of the other ANC leaders, too. More than twenty leaders, including Nelson, were jailed. But when they were released, the Defiance of Unjust Laws Campaign continued to operate. Until riots broke out in Cape Province.

A dozen people, both black and white, were killed. Albert Luthuli, a Zulu chief who was the new ANC president, and Nelson called off the campaign immediately.

The angry South African government banned the top leaders of the ANC, the black unions, and the Indian Congress. Banning meant that they could not travel outside their township. They could not meet with groups of people. They could not write books or newspaper or magazine articles. And they could not speak on the radio. Over the years, the list of forbidden activities grew.

Just before he was banned, Nelson had been elected president of the Transvaal chapter of the ANC. But he was not allowed to go to the meeting at which he was supposed to take office. Someone else had to read the speech he wrote. In it Nelson promised that one day all the people of South Africa would gain equality. But, he warned, it would not be "an easy walk to freedom."

When leaders were banned, the people who were elected to replace them were also banned. Nelson began to worry about what his angry people might do without good leaders to guide them.

Living as a banned person was almost like living in a cell without bars. Wherever Nelson went, he was followed by police. From 1952 through 1961, he was almost always under banning orders.

Nelson had managed to complete law

Nelson Mandela in his law office in 1952.

school in 1952 and start a law practice with Oliver Tambo in Jo'burg. Even though the banning order made it difficult to work, Nelson always had clients. Many people had legal problems with the government. It seemed that there was no end to troubles in the racially divided nation of South Africa.

7

The Freedom Charter

Nelson and the ANC started working with many other South African organizations to draw up a Freedom Charter. First, ordinary people were asked questions such as "How would you make South Africa a happy place for all the people?" The Freedom Charter was based on their answers to these questions.

On June 25, 1955, about 3,000 people gathered in a soccer field at Kliptown, near Johannesburg, to adopt the charter. This historic meeting was called the Congress of the People.

Young and old, poor and well-off came from near and far. Although the government had been invited to participate, it sent only police detectives.

Since Nelson was banned, he could not attend without risking arrest. But Nelson was clever. He had learned to disguise himself. One day he would be a window washer, another day a clergyman or a chauffeur in a trim uniform. He disguised himself again to join with the people for this remarkable event.

The Freedom Charter begins with these words: "We the people of South Africa declare for all our country and the world to know: that South Africa belongs to all who live in it, black and white.... Our people have been robbed of their birthright to land, liberty, and peace."

The charter was divided into ten sections, which spoke of basic democratic rights to the vote, work, health care, education, and housing. After discussion, the people adopted each section by raising their hands and shouting out "Afrika!"

On the second afternoon of the meeting, police suddenly put up blockades and announced that no one could leave. Long into the night, the police checked passbooks and searched people. They took everyone's official papers and photographed the white delegates. Finally someone in the tired crowd started singing "Nkosi Sikelel' iAfrika," or "God Bless Africa." And the people kept on singing until the police finished.

In December 1956, Nelson Mandela and 155 others were charged with violently trying to overthrow the government—a crime punishable by death. Among those arrested were many blacks and some whites and Asians.

The accused were taken to court and put into a huge wire cage in the courtroom. Someone had put a sign on the cage that read DON'T FEED. The judge was outraged to see the sign and released the prisoners on bail.

Meanwhile, supporters were waiting outside the courthouse. They carried signs and sang "Nkosi Sikelel' iAfrika" and other hymns.

Suddenly, the police fired to force the crowd to leave. Twenty-two people were wounded, and world attention was drawn to South Africa. And so was money to pay for the expenses of the accused.

Even though Mandela could live at home, he had to report to the police station every other day. His law practice suffered, and so did his marriage. Sadly, it finally ended in divorce.

The trial dragged on while the government prepared its case. Life was not easy for the accused. They had to be ready at any time to appear in court. Because of this, some lost their jobs or their businesses. Many were far from their homes and families. And because there were no hotels for nonwhites, the accused were forced to move from one crowded house to another.

Nelson stayed in shape by boxing during his first treason trial in 1957.

But the government had done something that had been nearly impossible for the ANC to do. It had brought ANC leaders from all over the country to one place for a long time. And during that period, these leaders were able to exchange ideas and make plans.

In September 1957, charges were finally dropped against most of the accused, including Oliver Tambo and Chief Albert Luthuli. But Nelson and Walter were among twenty-seven people who were scheduled to go on trial in Pretoria in December 1958.

Around this time, Mandela met a beautiful young woman. She had just earned a degree in social work. Turning down a scholarship to the United States, she became the first black social worker at a Soweto hospital. Her Xhosa name was Nomzano. "Nomzano" means both "she who strives" and "she who will face trials." But everyone called her by her Christian name, Winnie.

Because Nelson was still under a banning order, there was little time for courtship. But Nelson knew he wanted Winnie for his wife, and she wanted him as her husband.

Nelson warned Winnie that being his wife would not be easy. And it took some work to convince Winnie's father to let her marry Nelson. But finally a date was set, and the government allowed Nelson a few days to go

Nelson and Winnie, a month before their wedding.

to Pongoland, Winnie's place of birth, for their wedding.

Nelson and Winnie were married in the Methodist church on June 14, 1958. Nelson's sister Leabie was one of three bridesmaids. After the Christian service, a praise singer took over. Wearing tribal robes of animal skins, he sang the praises of both Winnie's and Nelson's clans.

The wedding party went to Winnie's

ancestral burial grounds for a traditional feast and celebration. And after a party for the villagers at the town hall, the couple dashed back to Johannesburg.

For many years Winnie kept part of their wedding cake. She hoped that one day they could also celebrate their marriage with the elders of Nelson's family.

The couple lived in Soweto with luxuries few homes in the black township had—electricity and an indoor bathroom. They lived on Winnie's small salary, since Nelson had to travel to Pretoria every day once the treason trial began again.

The trial dragged on. New rules and regulations made life harder and harder for blacks. And this caused a split in the ANC. Many still believed in a society of racial equality. But now some of these same people felt that blacks had to act independently of whites. So in 1959 a man named Robert Sobukwe started a new group, the Pan-Africanist Congress (PAC). He soon set about planning a nationwide nonviolent protest.

On March 21 protesters turned in their passbooks all over the country. Of course, they were arrested. The PAC's hope was that the jails would become so full that the government would decide to get rid of the pass laws.

But the huge crowds in one township, Sharpeville, scared the police. Shots rang out. Protesters tried to run. The police shot volley after volley. When they finally stopped, sixty-nine unarmed people lay dead. And many more, including children, were wounded.

After this, the ANC forgot its differences with the PAC. Nelson and Luthuli burned their passbooks. Protests broke out all over the country.

The hideous pictures of the Sharpeville massacre were in newspapers around the world. Once again, the United Nations spoke out officially against South Africa. And once again, the world community was shocked.

*Soweto, the township where Nelson and Winnie
lived with their family.*

But the government didn't care. Prime
Minister Hendrik Verwoerd declared a state
of emergency. He banned both the ANC and
the PAC. All the leaders were arrested except
one, Oliver Tambo. He had slipped out of
the country to continue the work of the ANC
abroad.

Police raided people's homes. They went
through their possessions as if they were
worthless.

51

Nelson was put in the Pretoria prison. The state of emergency allowed the government to jail anyone for as long as it wished. No charges were necessary.

This time, Mandela acted as his own lawyer at the treason trial. He gave careful answers to the judge and to the government prosecutors. He cross-examined government witnesses. He knew the facts, and he knew the law.

Finally, in March 1961, the judge delivered his verdict in the treason trial. The government had not proved that the Freedom Charter called for a Communist state. This had been one of its main charges. And it had not proved that the ANC or the defendants had ever followed a violent policy. After more than five long years, the verdict was not guilty!

8

Sabotage!

Two situations finally convinced Mandela that there was no more hope for change through nonviolence. First, angry that the Queen of England had spoken out against its policies, the government left the British Commonwealth of Nations. South Africa became an independent republic on May 16, 1961.

When Nelson heard that this was about to happen, he wrote to Prime Minister Verwoerd and urged him to write a color-free constitution. Verwoerd ignored the letter.

Next, the government began shipping blacks to places called "independent homelands," or Bantustans. These were overcrowded, dry regions in the countryside where blacks were forced to live. It was nearly impossible to farm the soil in these areas, for it had been destroyed by too many people with too many goats and cattle.

It was also nearly impossible to earn money in the homelands. And there were no government services.

The government appointed chiefs of the homelands instead of letting the people choose them. The chiefs were rewarded with money and power, which caused many of them to side with the government or become corrupt. If the people rebelled against the choice of chiefs, the government would send in troops.

A good friend of Nelson's became the chief of the Transkei region. And Winnie's father accepted a post as the head of Pongoland. Nelson and Winnie saw both of them as traitors.

In October 1961, ANC president Luthuli

was awarded the Nobel Peace Prize. The government spoke out against the prize, but Luthuli was allowed to go to Norway to receive it.

But prize or no prize, the ANC was cornered. Every nonviolent means of protest was outlawed. Nelson and other leaders feared that, with no outlet for their anger, the people would become terrorists. Some leaders felt the answer now was guerrilla warfare.

Nelson was against this. He convinced the others that sabotage, or destruction of property, was the best route to take. Sabotage was violent. But it would hurt the economy, instead of human lives.

Mandela became the commander of a separate armed ANC organization, Umkhonto we Sizwe (Spear of the Nation). The targets would be power plants, phone lines, and railways—*never* people.

Using his disguises, Mandela traveled all over South Africa to sign up volunteers. A white friend let Mandela use his farm in

Rivonia, near Johannesburg, as a base.

In December 1961, the anniversary of the Blood River massacre, the Spear struck. Bombs went off in power plants in Johannesburg and Port Elizabeth. One volunteer was killed by the bomb he was trying to set off. Another lost an arm.

The Spear issued a statement that said the ANC always tried to achieve freedom by peaceful means. But it had reached the point where "there remain only two choices: submit or fight. That time has now come to South Africa."

The government stepped up its search for Mandela. It offered rewards in black newspapers. One time Nelson slid down a rope from the second story of a building while the police were downstairs.

Another time he pretended to be a night watchman. A black policeman walked straight toward him. This is it, thought Nelson. But the policeman gave him the thumbs-up ANC sign and passed him without saying a word.

Nelson Mandela was becoming a legend to South Africans. And he was becoming an embarrassment to the government. They just couldn't seem to catch him. From time to time he even had short visits with Winnie and their children, usually at the farm in Rivonia. His life as a fugitive was hard on all of them. Yet his daughters Zeni and Zinzi have happy memories of playing with him among the apple trees at the farm.

In January 1962, Nelson slipped out of the country to meet Oliver Tambo and speak at the Pan-African Freedom Conference in Ethiopia. He asked the nations of the world to continue their support. Many were already giving refuge to South Africans who had escaped. And many were not buying the country's exports.

The government was furious when Mandela's visits to other African countries and then to London were reported in the world press.

For Nelson, life outside South Africa was a new experience. "Wherever I went, I was treated like a human being." It was thrilling to see all races "mingling peacefully and happily." How tempting it must have been to remain abroad as a famous leader in exile. But Nelson's loyalty to his family and to his people drew him back home.

When Nelson returned, he spent a few days at the farm with his younger son, Makgatho.

Thembi, Nelson's older son, acted as his father's messenger. He risked his life carrying plans from Rivonia to Spear members.

One night a friend was driving Nelson home from a party at the farm. Police stopped the car and arrested him. He was charged with leaving the country without permission and inciting the people to strike. Nelson was not pleased to be arrested, but he was relieved that Rivonia had not been discovered.

Again Nelson served as his own lawyer. In cross-examining government witnesses, he asked why his letter to the prime minister was never answered. He said it was a scandal that the head of state refused to respond to a letter written on behalf of the majority of the population.

Mandela said that it had not been easy for him to "take up the life of a hunted man. I was driven to this situation, and I do not regret having taken the decisions I did take."

Nelson was sentenced to five years in prison. After a few months at Pretoria Central Prison, he was moved to Robben Island with three other black prisoners.

Robben Island is off the tip of the cape. In winter it's battered by harsh winds. In summer it broils beneath the sun. Only one prisoner, a tribal chief, ever escaped alive from Robben Island. And that happened almost 300 years ago.

Meanwhile, signs reading FREE MANDELA appeared in black townships and on college campuses in other parts of the world. And the Spear continued to strike.

9

Rivonia

It is late at night on July 11, 1963. A bakery truck and a cleaning van drive quietly onto the grounds of the Rivonia farm. Heavily armed police and attack dogs charge through the front door. The police trap Walter Sisulu, among others. But even worse, they find papers with maps and details. They now have proof that Nelson Mandela has been involved with the Spear.

Nelson was brought from Robben Island to Pretoria Central Prison and jailed with his political friends. They were shocked to see him. His skin had yellowed, and he had lost forty pounds. The dust from the limestone he hammered all day at Robben Island had affected his eyes. Yet Nelson still had his dignified and confident manner. And being with his friends was like taking vitamins. He gained weight and began to look like the old Nelson again.

Some of the best lawyers in the country offered to defend the accused without even knowing their names. But not until the day before the trial were they allowed to visit their clients and discover who they were.

Nelson knew the government had a solid case against him. But he also knew that the world press and international observers would be in the courtroom. So he decided to use the trial to show the world the true face of the government rather than to fight for his own life. This decision made him feel better.

In fact, Nelson never seemed to lose his sense of humor or his intelligence. One day a guard named Swanepol saw Nelson frown and hand someone a note. The prisoners often wrote each other notes, since the guard could hear every word they said. But, after reading the notes, they always quickly crumpled them and burned them in an ashtray.

This note was clearly a secret. The prisoner crumpled it up. But he didn't burn it. Swanepol grabbed the note, saying it might start a fire. His face turned red when he read Nelson's note. It said, "Isn't Swanepol a fine-looking chap?"

Nothing could break Nelson's spirit. In fact, he even took some tests during a recess before the judge gave his verdict. Nelson was trying to get an advanced law degree by mail from London University. And he passed the tests!

But before the recess, Nelson spoke to the court for four hours. He spoke of family life, which was breaking down under even harsher pass laws and banning orders. One banned person could not talk to another, even if they were married. He reminded people that instead of living with their families, fathers had to live miles away in worker hostels. Children got by however they could with hardly any schools to attend. Violence and robberies were turning black townships into danger zones.

Nelson ended with these words: "During my lifetime I have dedicated myself to the struggle of the African people. I have fought against white domination, and I have fought against black domination. I have cherished the ideal of a democratic and free society in which all people live together in harmony and with equal opportunities. It is an ideal which I hope to live for and achieve. But if it needs be, it is an ideal for which I am prepared to die."

The judge gave his verdict on June 11, 1964. He pronounced all but one of the defendants guilty. They would be sentenced the next day.

Before dawn a crowd gathered in front of the courthouse. They carried signs and banners expressing pride in their leaders. One sign read, NO TEARS: OUR FUTURE IS BRIGHT.

Winnie Mandela and Nelson's mother outside the courthouse where Nelson was found guilty of treason.

But everyone knew that the punishment for these crimes could be death.

A hush filled the courtroom as the judge spoke. He had chosen to go easy on the prisoners. Instead of death, the sentence was life imprisonment.

Mandela gave his mother and Winnie the thumbs-up ANC sign and a smile. He was ready to start his life as Prisoner 446/64. And this time the government would give him a new suit—a thin shirt and short pants.

Imagine what it must be like to be locked alone in a cement cell. It is seven feet wide by seven feet long. There is no bed, just two blankets. There is no drinking water except at meals. You may not sing or even pray aloud. You may not speak to other prisoners. And if you're caught speaking to the man gathering seaweed beside you, you'll be punished. Your family is over 1,000 miles away.

Imagine life on Robben Island as Prisoner 446/64.

10

Robben Island

It's hard to believe the rules for serving food on Robben Island. The *same* cornmeal was prepared differently for each racial group on *different* days. Colored and Asian prisoners could have one spoonful of sugar and bread with their breakfast porridge. The blacks could have half a spoonful of sugar—and no bread!

Nelson may have laughed at that practice. But the isolation was no laughing matter. He was not allowed to see a newspaper. Had the world forgotten his people? For years, bits of news from recently arriving

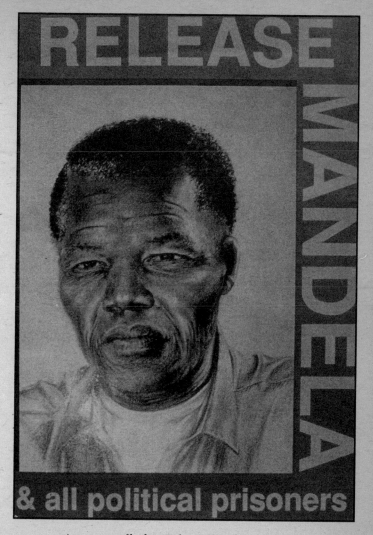

A poster calls for Nelson Mandela's release.

prisoners were the only way Nelson knew what was happening in his country.

And how he missed his family! He was rarely permitted to write home or to receive letters. Letters could be no longer than 500 words, and they could not discuss politics.

Prisoners were allowed two visits a year. Winnie Mandela and Albertina Sisulu were given permission to visit their husbands at the same time. But since both women were banned, they had to make the long, costly trip separately.

Visits lasted only half an hour. Visitors and prisoners looked at each other through a small closed window and spoke over a phone. And of course, a guard was always present to be sure politics was not discussed.

Within the jail, Nelson soon became a spokesman for the political prisoners. He put pressure on the prison authorities to improve living conditions. He organized work slow-downs and hunger strikes.

Little by little, living conditions improved

in small but important ways. The food was a bit better. Prisoners could have drinking water. And after some time they were allowed to exercise outside their cells, to plant gardens, and to study certain subjects by mail. (But law was *not* one of those subjects!) They could wear blankets in the winter while they read. And small desks were put in the cells.

As always, Nelson kept up his program of daily exercise and studied Afrikaans and economics. Most important, his good humor was catching. Even the guards began to like him. After a few years, they would sometimes leave newspapers where they knew he would find them.

As he changed conditions in the prison, Nelson also created a community among the prisoners. He encouraged them to study and discuss ideas. And because they could now study subjects by mail, they had some sort of hope for the future.

II

Growing Opposition

The outside world did not forget Nelson Mandela or the racism of his country. Schoolchildren, movie stars, rock stars, religious leaders—it seemed everyone was coming out against the racism of South Africa. And in 1974 the United Nations suspended South Africa from membership.

Within the country, new groups against apartheid sprang up. These included student groups, a white South African women's group, and many religious groups. Only the

South African Dutch Reformed Church was still in favor of apartheid.

British soccer teams had started protesting during the Rivonia trial. Soon athletes all over the world refused to play against South African teams. In 1964 South Africa was banned from the Olympics. South African athletes began thinking about their government's policies, and they didn't like them.

Apartheid hurt businesses as well. Many people began to refuse to buy South African exports or to invest their money in South African industries. And foreign companies began to refuse to export goods to South Africa.

Rich in almost every mineral except oil, South Africa was forced to import it. In 1973 African and Arab countries selling oil to South Africa stopped.

Finally, in 1986, the United States government made it illegal for the United States citizens or companies to invest money in South

African businesses or to import valuable materials from South Africa. It also became illegal for South African airlines to land in the United States. These actions are called economic sanctions.

At the same time, Great Britain and other European countries were taking similar actions against South Africa.

Meanwhile, black children were getting less and less schooling. The Bantu Education Bill had made it nearly impossible for black children to get even a basic education. This bill barred blacks from studying for many jobs—even those that had nothing to do with politics. High school and college were possible for only a few.

Unemployment caused miserable poverty in the homelands. At the same time, there was a growing shortage of skilled labor. Disgusted with apartheid, skilled whites had begun leaving the country. So some companies began to offer high school and college scholarships to black students. They desperately needed educated workers.

But the government did not want to help business by educating blacks. Instead, they tried to convince whites from countries like Poland to move to South Africa. In fact, the government now started to make it even harder for blacks to get the skills that business and industry needed.

To make matters worse, the way the National Party had set up election districts, it seemed they could never be voted out of office.

A young black medical student named Steve Biko started a movement called black consciousness in the late 1960s. Inspired by Nelson Mandela, he urged blacks to take pride in themselves—to have a can-do attitude.

Like Nelson Mandela, Biko put his words into action. He set up clinics to treat poor blacks in the countryside. He started projects to help black people help themselves by learning practical skills.

Biko's message was simple: Rely on yourself. Learn as much as you can. Help others. And naturally, Biko was banned. But just as Nelson Mandela's words continued to inspire the people, so did Biko's.

No one took Biko's words more seriously than the schoolchildren and teachers of Soweto.

In 1976 a law was passed saying that black schools must teach in Afrikaans rather than in English. Afrikaans is spoken only by Afrikaners in South Africa. It is the form of Dutch their ancestors spoke 300 years ago.

Hardly any teachers in Soweto knew Afrikaans. How could they teach in a language they didn't know? The law brought the students' rage to the boiling point.

Their leaders were either banned or in jail. But the students had to do *something*. So, carrying homemade signs, thousands of unarmed students filled the streets. Their spirits were high. They were determined to show how much education meant to them.

But suddenly, without warning, police started shooting into the crowd. Some students fell, but the rest of the children kept marching toward the police.

By noon Soweto was a war zone. Helicopters dropped tear gas from above. Policemen used high-powered weapons below. What started as a protest turned into a riot, one that lasted three days. When it was over, every government building or shop that was a symbol of apartheid was in ruins.

The first child to die was Hector Petersen, who was shot in the back. Hector was thirteen years old. A picture of another student carrying his bleeding body appeared on the front page of newspapers. It flashed across TV screens around the world. People were outraged and shocked.

Between 800 and 1,000 people died during those few days in Soweto. Among them was one white civilian, Dr. Melville Edelstein. He worked at a Soweto clinic and was on the side of black people. But the mob saw only his white skin. They stomped him to death.

While all this went on, Nelson was imprisoned on Robben Island without a TV or newspaper. It would take time for him to learn about Soweto. And when he did hear about what had happened, his heart ached for his country and for the children of Soweto—so poor, so angry, so wounded.

Nelson had warned the government about the possibility of great violence. But they had refused to listen.

12

Inside and Outside Prison Walls

In 1973, James Kruger, the minister of justice, police, and prisons, offered Nelson a deal. He would reduce Nelson's sentence if Nelson would support the homelands policy. Nelson refused to accept the deal. He would not betray his people.

Knowing that books were more important to Nelson than food, his jailers thought up a cruel punishment. A guard claimed that Nelson was writing his autobiography. This guard said he'd found proof. But no one would show Nelson what that proof was.

As punishment, Nelson and his fellow political prisoners were not allowed to study or read a book of any kind. For four long years, all they had to read were the few letters they received.

Nelson also found it very difficult being away from his family. He was not there to comfort his children and give them advice. Children between the ages of two and sixteen were not allowed to visit the prison. When Nelson was sent to Robben Island for the first time, Zeni was three and Zinzi was two.

While Nelson was in prison, his younger son, Makgatho, left school. Nelson wrote Makgatho a letter trying to convince him to stay in school. He told him how important an education was. But sending a letter wasn't the same as speaking in person.

Nelson's oldest daughter, Maki, had married, gotten divorced, and remarried. When his son Thembi was killed in a car crash, all Nelson could do was write to his first wife, Evelyn.

When Nelson's mother, Nosekeni Fanny, died, Winnie had to describe the funeral to him. The prison officials would not let Nelson attend.

There were happy times, too—birthdays, weddings, and graduations—but Nelson could celebrate them only by mail. In one of his letters to Winnie, he wrote these sad words: "Sometimes I feel like one who is on the sidelines, who has missed life itself."

But Nelson rarely complained. He wrote warm, loving letters to his children. He described the little things that brightened his life in jail—a bird he saw, a plant he grew. And he always encouraged his children. He was interested in what they were doing and thinking. Their pictures were his treasures.

On Nelson's sixtieth birthday, both friends and people he had never met sent letters and gifts. Yet he wasn't allowed to receive these gifts. But he did have a wonderful late birthday present.

His daughter Zeni was finally able to visit

This photo of Nelson Mandela, taken in 1990, was the
first photo of him published in over twenty years.

him in jail. She had married a prince of Swaziland, so by using diplomatic privileges, she was able to visit her father. Both Nelson and Zeni held back tears as they embraced. It was the first time Nelson had touched a member of his family in sixteen years. Then Zeni placed her newborn baby in his arms.

Zeni and her husband asked Nelson to name their baby. He named her Zaziwe, which means Hope.

Nelson worried most about Winnie. The police bothered Winnie endlessly. Her banning order made her life very difficult. She could not keep a job and was jailed so often that she kept a bag ready to take with her in case she had to leave at a moment's notice. At one point she was put in solitary confinement for 200 days.

Time after time, judges would find Winnie not guilty. The police would arrest her right in the courtroom and jail her again. But Winnie became more and more outspoken, especially for the rights of black South African women. She was no longer just Nelson Mandela's wife. She became known throughout the world for her own beliefs and actions.

At the same time, books, plays, and news reports about the horrors of South Africa were creating greater sympathy worldwide for nonwhite South Africans. This sympathy focused on one man—Nelson Mandela.

The world celebrated Nelson Mandela's seventieth birthday with a blockbuster concert, called Freedomfest, held at Wembley Stadium in London. Rock stars, opera singers, musicians in exile, and others performed before a crowd of 75,000 people. Millions more heard broadcasts of the concert. It lasted for more than eleven hours and ended with a spectacular display of fireworks.

Oliver Tambo and other ANC members were guests of honor. But Nelson Mandela, the real guest of honor, was far away.

All celebrations were banned in South Africa. Roadblocks were set up around the prison to keep people away. One family was having a birthday party at home. But the police arrived and stopped it.

Birthday greetings poured in—from the Pope, heads of state, famous entertainers, well-known athletes, and ordinary people. Schoolchildren in distant countries sang, "Happy birthday, Mr. Mandela." The greetings sent to Nelson were forwarded to his address in Soweto.

Mandela was forty-five years old when he went to prison for treason. How must he have felt when he turned seventy and was still behind bars?

13

Last Steps on a Long Road

As more and more angry young prisoners arrived at Robben Island, Nelson became their teacher. He prepared them to be the future leaders of a democratic and multi-racial country—a new South Africa. Nelson's self-control and commitment to study set an example.

Late one night in 1982, Nelson was moved in great secrecy along with Walter Sisulu and several other prisoners. They were taken to Pollsmoor, a modern prison near Cape Town.

It would take time for Nelson to realize why this move was made.

Pollsmoor was a better place to be in some ways. There was a library and a radio. But the political prisoners were kept together in one cell. And Nelson missed his garden and the sight of growing things. He complained about his health for the first time. Winnie knew that the best way to force the prison to make changes was to make Nelson's complaints public.

On May 12, 1984, Winnie and Nelson had a surprise. For the first time in twenty-two years, they were allowed to hug each other during a visit. And they could speak without a window of plastic between them.

But Nelson was still not feeling well. In 1985, he entered the Volks Hospital in Cape Town for surgery. Winnie had permission to see him. Since she was not allowed to drive or take trains out of her assigned area, she had to fly.

Kobie Coetsee, the new minister of justice, police, and prisons, was on the same flight. On his way to his first-class seat, Coetsee stopped in the economy section and spotted Winnie. He assured her that the government was concerned about her husband's health.

As soon as the plane was in the air, Coetsee found Winnie Mandela had taken the seat next to him. By the time they landed, Coetsee had made up his mind to visit Nelson.

So while Nelson was recovering, Coetsee visited him. Nelson acted like a good host. He introduced Coetsee to his nurses, as if he were a guest at a party. Coetsee was amazed by Nelson's dignity and easy humor. The top cop and the famous prisoner became friends.

Since he was a cabinet member, Coetsee often saw the new president of South Africa, P. W. Botha. Botha was so grumpy his staff called him "The Old Crocodile." But he didn't like the fact that South Africa had become "The skunk of the world," as Nelson called it. So Botha made some reforms. But none of them really made much difference in the lives of nonwhites. Nor did they make South Africa any more popular throughout the world.

South Africa had become a world outcast, while Nelson had become a world hero. Universities gave him honorary degrees. Honors and international awards were heaped upon him. Streets, schools, and parks were named after him. A British nuclear scientist discovered a new particle, which he named the Mandela particle.

When Nelson returned to Pollsmoor, he was given a large, comfortable cell. But this made him uneasy. He had always insisted on living just like any other political prisoner. He didn't want to be given special treatment.

Shortly after Nelson's return, Coetsee began making secret contacts with him and several exiled ANC leaders. Prison officials took Mandela for drives around Cape Town and even for walks along the beach. Mandela felt that they were preparing him for the outside world. But on what terms?

Nelson gradually came to understand why the government had moved him and the other ANC prisoners from Robben Island to Pollsmoor. Government officials wanted to have meetings with them and needed to have them nearby.

Throughout the world, more and more countries began refusing to do business with South Africa. They hoped that this would force the South African government to do away with apartheid. But the British Commonwealth countries were in disagreement over this. In 1986 they sent a group of seven people called the Eminent Persons Group to South Africa. These people were to meet with Nelson and report back on the meeting.

Coetsee wanted to show the group how well Nelson was treated. The prison tailor made a new suit for their star prisoner. He met with the group in the prison guest house.

Nelson made such a powerful impression that even the most conservative member of the group came out against apartheid and joined the cry: "Free Mandela!"

Back in January 1985, against the advice of Coetsee, Botha had already offered to free Nelson Mandela. But he would free him only if Nelson would make a public statement against violence. Nelson's lawyer flew to Pollsmoor to get his reply.

On February 10, 1985, crowds filled Jabulani Stadium in Soweto. Zinzi, Nelson's youngest daughter, then twenty-four years old, read her father's answer to Botha's offer. It was a loud and clear no.

More than half the people present had not been born yet when Nelson was sent to Robben Island. Yet his words thrilled them:

"Let him [Botha] renounce violence. Let him say he will dismantle apartheid. Let him unban ... the African National Congress. . . . Let him free all who have been imprisoned, banished, or exiled for their opposition to apartheid. . . .Too many have died since I went to prison. . . .Your freedom and mine cannot be separated. I *will* return."

Shortly after this, Nelson was hospitalized with tuberculosis, a serious lung disease. He was very ill. Many people throughout the world were deeply concerned. If Nelson Mandela died, what would become of South Africa?

With excellent care, Nelson slowly recovered in a comfortable house at Victor Verster Prison, thirty miles from Cape Town. He was allowed to have visitors. Even Robben Island and Pollsmoor prisoners were brought to see him.

While Nelson was getting better, violent conflicts were getting worse. Nelson knew he had to act.

He sent a letter to Botha. It restated the ANC position on equal voting rights. But it also said that a way had to be found to protect the rights of the white minority.

Botha wanted to meet with Nelson.

Once again the government bought Nelson a new suit. The meeting went very well. The Old Crocodile liked Nelson.

More meetings took place. Even some members of the Broederbond wanted changes. But the security forces warned Botha against a Communist takeover. In the end, nothing was changed.

Botha soon resigned under pressure. Frederik Willem de Klerk would be the new president. And de Klerk was even more in favor of apartheid than Botha!

Not surprisingly, the situation in South Africa continued to get worse. A state of emergency had been in effect since 1986. The police patrolled Soweto and other townships in armored cars. They searched, beat up, and arrested people at whim.

Unable to express their frustration and anger against such force, blacks turned against one another. Blacks who were suspected of supporting or spying for the government were beaten up by other blacks.

South Africa was becoming more and more lawless. The newspapers no longer even bothered to report most killings in the townships. But fortunately, de Klerk was proving to be a smart politician. He began to see that the only way to bring peace to his country would be to share power. Once he reached that decision, he acted boldly and opened talks with Nelson and the ANC.

Nelson was firm on several points: freeing political prisoners, giving voting rights to all South Africans, and lifting the ban on outlawed political parties. And Mandela, as always, had no wish to replace white domination with black domination.

De Klerk had no intention of agreeing to all of Nelson's demands. But Nelson had learned patience during all those years in prison. So he worked out a plan that de Klerk could accept.

It called for the democratic election of

a new government. And that government would be in charge of writing a new, democratic constitution.

Never once did Mandela ask for his own release from prison. His first concern was the release of Walter Sisulu and the other Rivonia prisoners. He wanted to make sure they were released before he was.

At dawn on October 10, 1989, a police car stopped in front of Walter's home. The seventy-seven-year-old man walked out of the car and through a door he had not entered in twenty-five years. He held his wife in his arms.

During this time other elderly prisoners were freed as well.

Joyful South Africans marched through the streets. They carried the banned ANC flag. They were not arrested, but they all had one question. When would Nelson Mandela be free?

14

Free at Last!

On February 2, 1990, President de Klerk made a speech that stunned Parliament. He announced that the bans on the ANC and sixty other groups, even the South African Communist Party, would be lifted. The state of emergency would end. Almost 400 political prisoners were to be freed, with executions temporarily halted.

And Nelson Mandela would be free—with no conditions!

Nine days later, the prison gates swung open. A stream of cars drove through them and stopped. A slim man with gray hair got out of a silver car. He smiled at the group of

*Nelson Mandela, with Winnie, finally leaving prison
for good on February 11, 1990.*

several hundred people standing in the sun-
shine. Then he raised his fist in the ANC
salute. The people were still cheering as Nelson Mandela got back in the car and drove
off toward Cape Town.

De Klerk was worried that the celebrations upon Nelson's release could turn into
riots. People were lining the main highway.

*Nelson Mandela waves to thousands of supporters
in Cape Town during his first public speech
after being released from prison in 1990.*

They hoped for a glimpse of their hero.

The cars took back roads to avoid the crowds. There were many stops along the way, but Nelson Mandela finally arrived at Cape Town's Grand Parade Stadium.

More than 100,000 people had been waiting for Nelson for over ten hours. A few angry young people had torn down the platform for the TV cameras and banged up a car. It was the car that the Reverend Jesse Jackson was using.

Reverend Jackson had worked with Martin Luther King, Jr., in the United States. He had spoken up for civil rights for South Africans for many years. Now he spoke to the crowd, trying to calm them. But by the time the police thought it was safe for Nelson to speak, many people had given up and gone home.

A few days later, a huge rally took place in Soweto. Over 120,000 people crammed into the city's soccer stadium. Almost that

Nelson speaks to more than 120,000 supporters in Soweto after his release from prison.

many waited outside. Nelson and several other ANC leaders arrived by helicopter. They were met by cheers as they stepped out of the helicopters and gave the ANC salute.

"We are going forward," Nelson told the people. He even called upon the police to "join our march to a new South Africa." As he finished speaking, green, gold, and black balloons floated up into the blue sky. Green, gold, and black are the colors of the ANC.

Nelson raised his fist to shouts of "Afrika!" Young people dressed in the ANC col-

The people of South Africa try to get a glimpse of Nelson Mandela as he returns home for the first time in twenty-seven years.

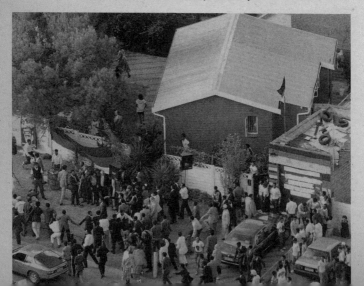

Nelson Mandela with the African National Congress group that met with the South African government in 1990. Walter Sisulu is in the front row, second from the right.

ors twirled batons on a platform. The rally was a huge success.

Finally a helicopter whisked Nelson away for a few quiet days at home. His grandchildren were waiting to see him.

Now that the ANC was no longer outlawed, its leaders returned from exile. The ANC began to become a political party. Nelson spent much of his time working with his old ANC friends and meeting the younger leaders. But he was so busy that his doctors

A man sells Nelson Mandela T-shirts to celebrate Nelson's 1990 visit to New York City.

worried. After so many years in prison, Nelson could not seem to get enough of his new-found freedom.

And the world could not get enough of Nelson Mandela. He went on a six-week tour to fourteen countries. He met with presidents and prime ministers. Everywhere he went, enthusiastic crowds greeted him.

In New York City, the Empire State Building was lit up with the ANC colors. There was a ticker-tape parade in his honor. Nelson was driven through the streets in a bullet-proof glass car. It was called the Mandela Mobile. The people could see him wave in answer to their cheers.

When he returned home, Nelson became involved in many issues that affected his government. There was so much to be done. And he was ready to do it. But when he spoke to the United Nations, he urged them to keep sanctions in place until the elections.

President Bush listens while Nelson Mandela gives thanks for U. S. support of the ANC.

His people were still not completely free.

Wherever Nelson Mandela went, celebrities and businesspeople made generous contributions to the ANC. He returned home full of energy. He was ready for the elections. And who would be running on the ANC ticket but Nelson Mandela himself.

As the elections began, voters flooded the polls. It was a joyful time for people around the world when black South Africans were finally allowed to cast their votes!

Nelson Mandela himself voted in a township high school. "This is an unforgettable occasion for all South Africans," he said. "We are starting a new era of hope."

By the end of the election, 10 million votes were in. The results were still being added up. But it was clear who the winner would be. "After so many centuries," said President de Klerk, "all South Africans are now free." He conceded the victory to Nelson Mandela, calling him a "man of destiny."

Nelson received the news at a hotel in

*Nelson Mandela, President F. W. de Klerk, and Zulu leader
Mangosuthu Buthelezi meet for peace talks in 1991.*

Johannesburg. He told his supporters, "I
stand before you filled with deep pride and
joy. Pride in the humble people of this country. Joy you can loudly proclaim from the
rooftops. Free at last!"

By May 2, all the votes—19 million!—
had been counted. Nelson Mandela was to
be the first black president of South Africa.

Mandela spoke at the ANC headquarters
in Johannesburg. He congratulated all the
parties he would be working with in a gov-

ernment of national unity. He asked all South Africans to tackle the country's problems. "Now is the time for all South Africans to celebrate the birth of a new South Africa," he said.

People of all races took his advice. Strangers danced together in the streets. In Soweto thousands of people danced and sang their way to Nelson Mandela's house. Many South Africans who had left their country started returning home. Their friends and loved ones greeted them with open arms.

President de Klerk said, "Mr. Mandela has walked a long road and now stands at the top of a hill. A traveler would sit down and admire the view. But a man of destiny knows that beyond this hill lies another. And another. The journey is never complete. As he contemplates the next hill, I hold out my hand to Mr. Mandela in friendship and cooperation."

At last inauguration day arrived. It was the day on which Nelson Mandela would officially become president. In the past these ceremonies had been stiff and formal. But Nelson's relaxed, easygoing style was catching. His inauguration was marked by a spirit of lively goodwill.

Thunderous applause greeted Nelson Mandela as he entered Parliament for the first time. He had chosen his own dark blue suit with a white rose.

Instead of taking his seat, Nelson walked across the floor. He shook hands with Chief Buthelezi, the leader of the Zulu party, Mr. de Klerk, and General Constand Viljoen, the leader of the Afrikaner Freedom Front.

Viljoen had been the head of the South African Defence Force in the 1980s. He was responsible for the deaths of many black Africans. But Nelson was determined to make his inauguration a time of healing and forgiveness.

South Africa's chief justice gave the new members of parliament (MPs) their oaths of office. One MP from the ANC was a young white woman, Melanie Verwoerd. Her hus-

After a lifetime of struggle, Nelson Mandela is sworn in as South Africa's first democratically elected president.

band's grandfather, Hendrik Verwoerd, had been the main founder of apartheid. But Melanie and her husband were working for racial equality.

The chief justice asked for nominations for the post of president. Albertina Sisulu, Walter's wife, had the great honor of nominating Nelson Mandela. No one opposed the nomination.

"Accordingly," said the chief justice, "I declare Nelson Rolihlahla Mandela to be the duly elected president of the Republic of South Africa."

Loud cheers answered his words.

When Nelson Mandela began to speak, there were smiles and tears on many faces. He said, "The time for the healing of wounds has come. The time to build is upon us." He pictured a society in which "all South Africans will be able to walk tall, without fear in their hearts—a rainbow nation at peace with itself and the world."

Economic sanctions were ended. The United Nations welcomed South Africa back into the global community.

As Nelson looked around the room, he may have thought of the fact that almost all of the ANC MPs had been political prisoners. Now lawbreakers would become lawmakers.

And the most famous prisoner of all, Nelson Mandela, had become the new president!

A white policeman and a black woman dance after Nelson Mandela is sworn in as South Africa's first democratically elected president.

15

President Mandela

President Mandela faces an enormous task. What problem shall he address first?

The nonwhites of South Africa are desperately in need of housing, health care, education, and jobs. The economy must be rebuilt. Afrikaner extremists want a *Volkstaat*, or independent state. And years of apartheid have left many old ideas that some will have trouble changing.

Nelson Mandela is confident that he and the new South Africa are up to the challenge. And the whole world agrees!

Bobbi Katz, a former children's-book editor, has published many children's poems and books. She also finds time to give poetry workshops in schools and colleges.

For years, Ms. Katz has been actively involved in the civil-rights movement. She was at one time education chairperson of her local branch of the National Association for the Advancement of Colored People and program chairperson of Arts in Action, an organization that brings blacks and whites together through the arts.

Ms. Katz divides her time between New York City and Port Ewen, New York.

Bullseye Biographies